DATE DUE

OCT 0 4 1995		
FEB 2 3 2002		
AUG 0 7 2012		
JUN 0 9 2016		
JUL 1 9 2016		
GAYLORD		PRINTED IN U.S.A.

Published in 1989 by Warwick Press,
387 Park Avenue South, New York, New York 10016.
First published in 1989 by Kingfisher Books Ltd.

Text copyright © Chris and Melanie Rice 1989.
Illustrations copyright © Grisewood & Dempsey Ltd. 1989.

Library of Congress Catalog Card No. 88-51430
ISBN 0-531-19056-0

Printed in Italy

I Like Painting

MELANIE & CHRIS RICE

WARWICK PRESS
New York/London/Toronto/Sydney
1989

Contents

Portraits *8*

Family Portraits *10*

Silhouettes *12*

Painting People *14*

Style *16*

Mixing Colors *18*

Opposite Colors *20*

Paint *22*

Applying Paint *24*

Action Painting *26*

Shapes in Pictures *28*

Arranging a Picture *30*

Perspective *32*

Line *34*

Pattern *36*

Paintings on Walls and Ceilings *38*

Working Together *40*

Paintings Everywhere *42*

Index *44*

Introducing Paintings

People have been painting for thousands of years all over the world—which adds up to a lot of paintings! Only a few fit into a book this size, so we have simply chosen some of our favorites. We hope you will like them too.

There is so much to look at in a painting, as you will soon realize. First you might notice a familiar face, an animal that you recognize, or a room like your own. Now take a second look. You will probably pick out something different—light shining through a window, a shadow, a baby crying perhaps. Take a closer look. Maybe you can pick out some brush strokes, or the painter's name scratched in a corner. Sometimes nothing in the picture looks familiar. There are no people, animals or buildings —just shapes or splashes of color. The painting seems to make no sense but it is good to look at, and your eye keeps going back to it. If you were to ask someone else to look at the same painting they may think differently about it, see different things in it. It doesn't matter: each person's reaction to a painting is his or her own.

When we wrote the book we wanted to tell you about the artists and how they painted. We also thought you might like to try out some things for yourself, so we've included some activity pages to start you off. Have fun!

Chris   Melanie

Portraits

A **portrait** is a picture of a person or group of people. Artists paint people as they see them, so two pictures of the same person can look very different.

Cathy drawn by Catherine.

Cathy drawn by Emmanuellar.

Edgar Degas: *L'Etoile (The Star)*.

Marc Chagall: *Les Noces (The Wedding)*.

Portraits often tell us something about the person (**subject**) being painted. Look at these paintings by Edgar Degas and Marc Chagall. The subject of the Degas is a ballerina and the Chagall shows some musicians. Some portraits leave us guessing. Who is the lady in Leonardo da Vinci's painting and what is she smiling about? No one knows.

Leonardo da Vinci: *Mona Lisa*.

What do you think?

The young man (*below*) could be happy, sad, sulky, or bored. It is difficult to tell what he is thinking about or what his feelings are. The picture (*right*) is called *Kit's Writing Lesson*. Do you think the boy is working hard? Master Lambton, in *The Red Boy*, doesn't look very comfortable posing for the artist. See how long you can sit in this position without moving.

Robert Martineau: *Kit's Writing Lesson*.

Domenico Ghirlandaio: *Portrait of a Young Man*.

Thomas Lawrence: *The Red Boy (Master Lambton)*.

Family Portraits

Look at the details in these two portraits of families. See if you can work out from the painting what they are like and how they spend their time together.

Jan Steen: *The Dancing Lesson.*

Can you find?

The man in the window.

The cat.

The dog.

The handle.

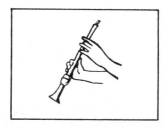

The instrument.

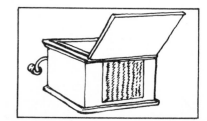

The musical box.

Catherine Rice: *My Family*.

Draw a portrait of your own family. Put in details which tell what you think is special about the people in your family, and which show the things they like doing when they are together.

William Hogarth: *The Graham Children*.

Silhouettes

A **silhouette** is a shape colored black, like a shadow.

Some artists use silhouettes to add interest to their paintings. In Rembrandt's portrait the light shines on the baby and his father, but the mother is in silhouette.

Rembrandt van Rijn: *The Holy Family*.

Can you find the silhouettes of a man in a doorway on pages 16 and 17 and another silhouette on page 21?

1 **To make a silhouette portrait**
Fasten a piece of paper to the wall.

2 Shine a light on the paper. Stand in front of the light: your shadow will now appear on the paper.

3 Ask a friend to draw around the outline of your shadow.

4 Fill in the outline with thick black paint.

Paint an interesting frame for your silhouette, or you could try cutting the silhouette out and mounting it onto colored paper.

Painting People

If you look at someone from the side, you can see their **profile**. Part of them is hidden from view. You can see only half of their face, part of an eye, one ear, and so on.

Seen face on, much more of the person is visible. You can see both eyes, ears, hands, and legs — but not the back of their head!

Egyptian artists chose to paint not what they could see, but what they wanted us to see. As you can see in the painting of Goldsmiths and Joiners, and of Hunefer, the figures are painted in profile, but their eyes are drawn as if from the front, and their bodies arranged so that both hands and both legs can be seen.

Hunefer.

Goldsmiths and Joiners.

Pablo Picasso: *Weeping Woman.*

The modern Spanish painter, Pablo Picasso, uses some of the Egyptians' ideas in his work. The painting *Weeping Woman* shows the sadness in the woman's eyes, as well as in her down-turned mouth and nose being dabbed by a handkerchief.

Caravaggio's people, on the other hand, are painted in a very realistic way, making the painting look more like a photograph. He uses light and shade to make his people look solid. Their hands and arms seem real enough to touch.

Caravaggio (Michelangelo Merisi): *The Supper at Emmaus.*

Style

Artists usually sign their pictures, but they write their names in different ways. Here are some artists' **signatures**. Can you find their paintings in this book?

The way an artist paints is as personal as his signature. Each artist has an individual **style**, or way of painting.

The painting by Diego Velazquez shows the Infanta (princess) Margarita Teresa and her maids. He has put himself in the picture. Can you see him?

Diego Velazquez: *Las Meninas (The Maids of Honor)*.

Pablo Picasso: *Las Meninas*.

Now look at the painting by Pablo Picasso. He has painted exactly the same subject but in his own style. Picasso is more interested in shapes than in making the picture seem real.

Can you find?

The artist's palette.   The man in the doorway.

The Infanta Margarita Teresa.   The dog.

Mixing Colors

White light is really a mixture of colors. If you break up a ray of white light you always find the same six colors in the same order. They are called the **spectrum**.

Alex Rice: *Traffic Jam*.

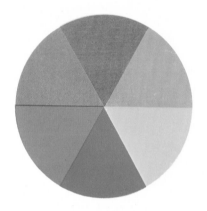

Red, yellow, and blue are the three **primary** colors. They can be mixed to make all the other colors. See how many different colors you can mix.

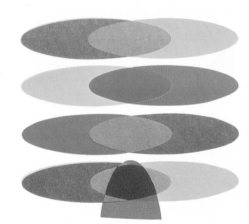

To make white
Cut out a circle of card. Paint on the colors of the spectrum as shown. Thread a piece of wool through two holes in the card. Hold the wool firmly at one end and twist the other end as much as you can. Now pull the wool sharply. When the circle spins quickly the colors seem to turn into white.

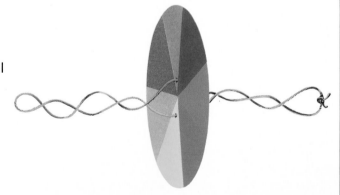

Georges Seurat: *Un Dimanche d'Eté à l'Ile de la Grande Jatte (A Sunday in the Summer at the Grande Jatte)*.

If you look closely at Georges Seurat's painting, you will see that it is made up of tiny dots or points of different colors crowded together. See if you can make your own picture of an umbrella, just using dots.

Opposite Colors

Opposite colors on the spectrum look stronger when they are placed next to one another.

Look at these three squares. Which is the brightest red? Actually they are all the same. Number 3 looks the brightest because it has been placed beside green, its opposite color on the spectrum.

Franz Marc likes to use opposite colors in his paintings. His blue horse stands out clearly against its red and yellow background. See what happens (*right*) when the horse is set against green and purple.

Franz Marc: *Blue Horse 1.*

Experiments with color

Experiment with colors yourself. Make these patterns or some of your own. Use opposite colors and colors that blend.

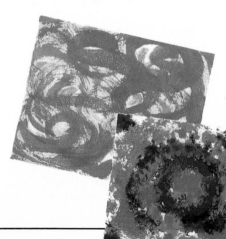

James Whistler uses pale colors, which blend together, to emphasize the girl's grace and beauty.

James Whistler: *Symphony in White No. 1: The White Girl.*

There is nothing hazy about this painting by Mary Cassatt. She makes use of strong bright colors to catch the eye.

Mary Cassatt: *The Boating Party.*

Paint

Jan van Eyck at work.

Artists usually paint onto a piece of canvas stretched over a wooden frame. This is fastened to a stand called an easel. They mix their colors on a palette.

Jan van Eyck: *Giovanni Arnolfini and his Bride*.

In the past, painters could not buy tubes, tins, or jars of paint—they had to make their own. They used colored plants and soft rocks such as chalk. These were crushed and mixed with oil.

Jan Vermeer: *The Artist's Studio*.

The Tale of Genji.

In Japan Keisai Eisen painted his picture onto silk. Other artists used ink and watercolor paints to give soft, washy colors.

Keisai Eisen: *Portrait of a Young Woman.*

Can you find?

Jan Vermeer, Keisai Eisen and the artist of *The Tale of Genji* have all used thin, delicate brushstrokes to paint small details on their paintings. See if you can find these details.

Applying Paint

Compare these three artists with those on the previous two pages. They paint using larger, bolder brushstrokes. Can you pick out the patterns their brushes have made on the canvas?

Berthe Morisot: *Jeune Fille en Blanc (Young Girl in White)*.

Auguste Renoir: *Luncheon at the Boating Party*.

Vincent van Gogh: *Portrait of Dr. Gachet*.

Activity

Brushes come in many shapes and sizes—try some out to make strokes of different thicknesses.

Pieces of sponge and balls of crumpled paper both make different patterns. They are useful for covering large areas of paper or canvas. Try mixing several colors.

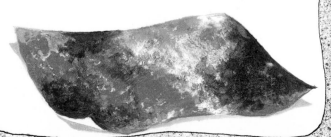

Spray painting (Spread out some newspaper first to catch the splashes.)

Cut out a shape from a piece of cardboard. Lay it on a piece of paper.
Dip a toothbrush into the paint.

Hold the handle with the bristles upright. Scrape your finger across the brush, toward you.
Paint will spray onto the paper.

Now move the shape and spray the paper with a new color.

Action Painting

An American artist, Jackson Pollock, thought up many new ways of applying paint. He laid his canvas on the floor and dripped, poured, or threw the paint on.

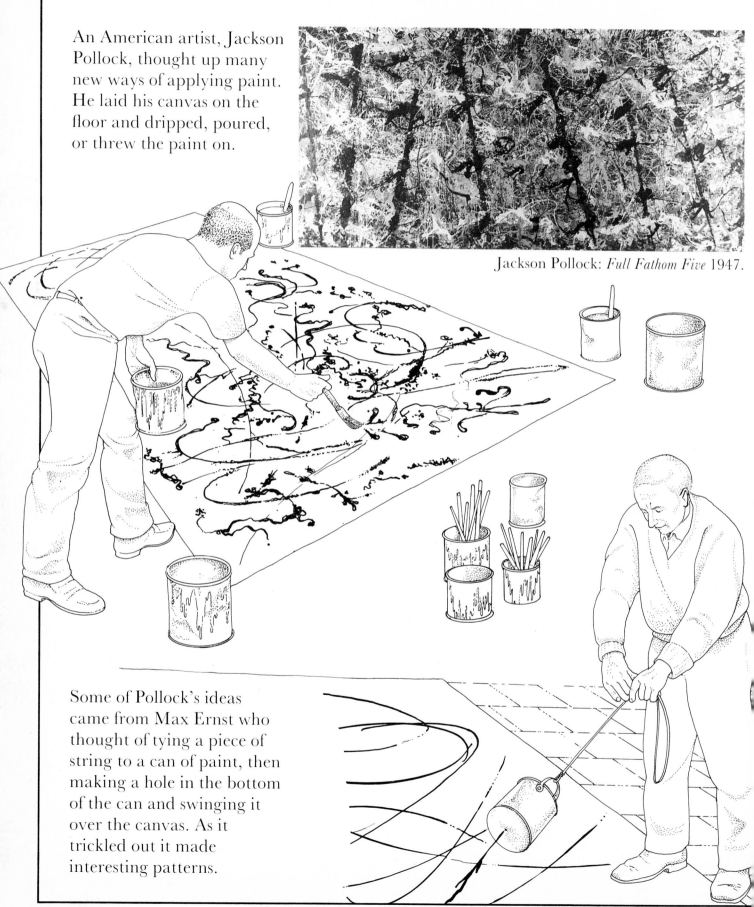

Jackson Pollock: *Full Fathom Five* 1947.

Some of Pollock's ideas came from Max Ernst who thought of tying a piece of string to a can of paint, then making a hole in the bottom of the can and swinging it over the canvas. As it trickled out it made interesting patterns.

Activity

Put a little runny paint into a plastic bag. Tie the bag with a piece of string. Make a small hole in one corner. Swing it over your sheet of paper.

1 Mix flour or wallpaper paste with powder paint to make a thick texture. Spoon a blob of paint onto the paper. Spread it around with your fingers. You can use cardboard combs and sticks to make patterns too.

2 Smear wallpaper paste over a piece of paper, then sprinkle on some powder paints and spread with your hands.

3 Take a print of your painting by placing a sheet of white paper over the top and pressing down firmly. Peel the print off carefully.

Use a drinking straw to blow drops of watery paint over the paper. Now fold the paper in half and press the two sides together.

Shapes in Pictures

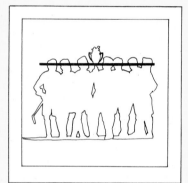

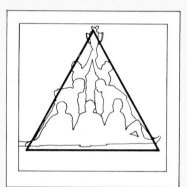

Artists arrange the people and objects in their paintings in a way that draws our attention to what is important.

In the first picture the team is arranged in a straight line and our eyes move along the line of heads. In the second picture the team is shown in a different arrangement. The figures are arranged so as to draw our eyes toward the cup. Look at the two pictures again. Decide which you think is more exciting.

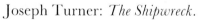

Joseph Turner: *The Shipwreck*.

Turner uses a spiral arrangement to capture the movement of the swirling sea.

Raphael (Raffaelo Sanzio): *The Virgin Mary with her Child and St. John the Baptist.*

Raphael arranges his subject in the shape of a triangle pointing up toward the face of the Virgin Mary.

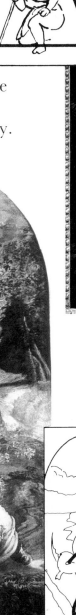

Jacopo Tintoretto arranges his picture along a wavy line to create a sense of movement and excitement.

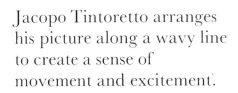

Jacopo Tintoretto: *St. George and the Dragon.*

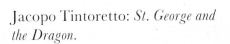

Arranging a Picture

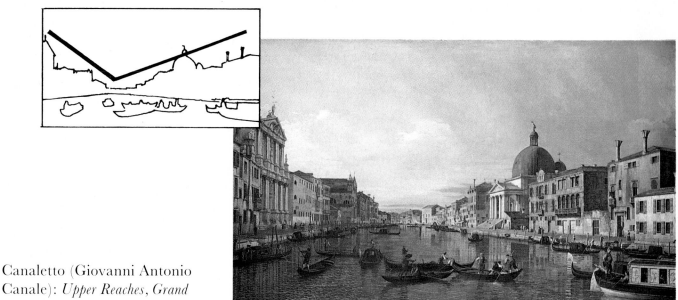

Canaletto (Giovanni Antonio Canale): *Upper Reaches, Grand Canal, Venice.*

The way the imaginary lines meet in the middle of these two pictures make us feel we can see a long way into the distance.

Meindert Hobbema: *The Avenue, Middelharnis.*

Pieter Bruegel has filled his canvas to bursting point with children playing. Some games even spill over the edge of the picture. See if you can pick out any games that you play with your friends.

Pieter Bruegel (the Elder):
Children's Games.

Can you find?

Whips and spinning-tops.

Leap frog.

Marbles.

Walking on stilts.

Dressing up.

Follow-the-leader.

Perspective

"Johannes": View of Venice

When we look at things in the distance, they seem smaller than they really are.

Hold up your thumb. It seems bigger than everything else in the room but of course it is not. It only looks bigger because it is nearer to you.

This is a painting of Venice. The artist has made no attempt to show distances: the people and objects in the background are the same size as those closest to us. The picture looks flat and there is no sense of **perspective**.

How do artists show perspective?
  Look at the picture by Antoine Watteau opposite. It can be divided into three parts:

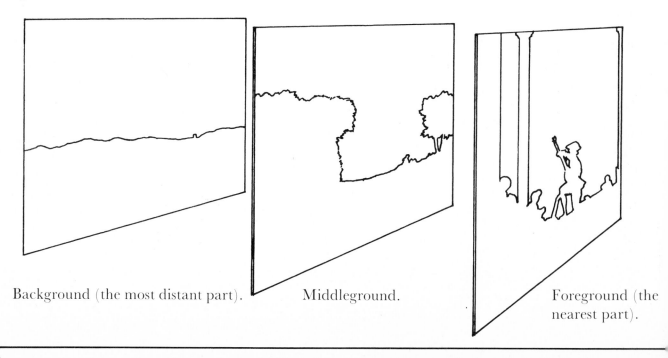

Background (the most distant part).   Middleground.   Foreground (the nearest part).

Can you find?

Here are five ways in which the artist shows perspective:

1. The imaginary lines move toward a point in the distance.

2. Nearby people are made bigger than those in the distance.

3. One object hides part of another, more distant one.

4. Distant objects are painted in paler, more blurred colors.

5. Nearby objects are painted in stronger colors and clearer detail.

Antoine Watteau: *The Charms of Life*.

33

Line

Some artists use lines to express feeling. Look at the way in which the words below describe a line. Choose the ones you think best describe the lines in Francis Picabia's painting.

Lines can be:

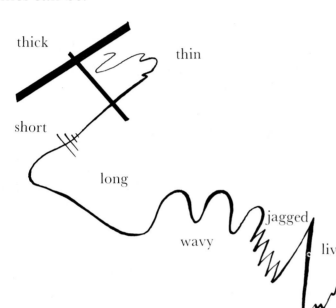

thick

thin

short

long

wavy

jagged

lively

strong

hard

gentle

curvy

soft

dotted

Francis Picabia: *Tickets annulès (Canceled Tickets).*

Lines can also describe shapes and things:

Dancing line

Find some music on the radio or put on your favorite record or tape. Let your paintbrush "dance" across the paper, making lines and shapes to "describe" the music.

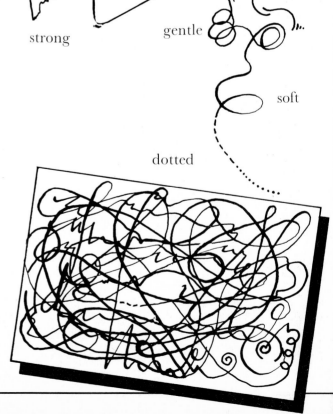

Look for lines in objects around you:

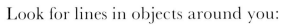

Tyrrel Broadbent builds his picture using blocks of color and line patterns.

Tyrrel Broadbent: *Conversation Piece*.

Can you find?

Pattern

This Indian artist uses lines to pattern everything in his painting: people, their clothing, the horses, the walls of the city, even the leaves on the trees.

The Siege of Fort Chitur.

Can you find?

The horses.

The riders.

The canopy.

The tree.

Maurits Escher has made a mosaic using shapes from his imagination as well as real things. How many black shapes can you see? How many white?

Maurits Escher: *Mosaic II.*

Can you find?

The frog.

The turtle.

Answer: 21 black, 19 white.

Paintings on Walls and Ceilings

People have been painting for at least 15,000 years. The earliest known painters used black and red pigments, made from soot, charcoal, and red rocks to draw on the walls of their caves.

Painting of a bison from a cave in Altamira, north Spain.

This Minoan painting was completed about 3,500 years ago. It was painted on the wall of a palace and shows the sport of bull-jumping.

Minoan wall painting from the palace in Knossos, Crete.

This modern wall painting brightens up a city street in Bolivia, South America. It was painted by schoolchildren.

Wall painting in La Paz, Bolivia, South America

Michelangelo: *Creation of Adam* (from the ceiling of the Sistine Chapel).

Painting a ceiling is never easy! One of the greatest ceiling paintings can be seen in the Sistine Chapel in Rome. It took the artist Michelangelo four years to complete. This is how it was done. Each detail was carefully planned first before being sketched out onto paper. Next the artist pricked holes around the lines of his sketch. He then laid out the sketch (called a cartoon) against the ceiling and dabbed black chalk through the holes. When he removed the paper the dotted outlines of the picture were left on the ceiling for him to fill in with paint.

Working Together

These children are working together on one large painting. Many great artists worked in studios with the help of assistants.

Peter Paul Rubens sometimes produced only a small colored sketch of a painting. His pupils and assistants had the task of copying this onto a large canvas and doing most of the painting themselves. Only then would Rubens step in to correct any mistakes and finish the finer details!

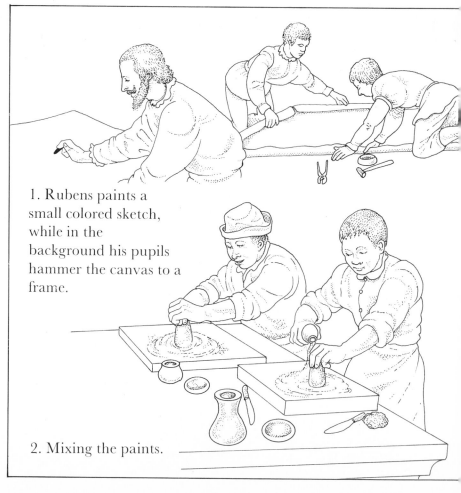

1. Rubens paints a small colored sketch, while in the background his pupils hammer the canvas to a frame.

2. Mixing the paints.

Peter Paul Rubens: *A Roman Triumph*.

3. Rubens' assistant paints onto the canvas.

4. Rubens applies the finishing touches.

Paintings Everywhere

Painting can be a job as well as a pleasure. Professional artists sell their paintings for money . . .

on the street . . .

. . . or at auctions.

Anyone can buy them, so a painting can end up almost anywhere . . . .

a palace . . .

in a church . . .

a private house . . .

or an art gallery.

But the original can be very expensive, so most people buy copies (prints) from shops.

Make your own gallery
Try painting a portrait of a
friend or a member of your
family.

Use a wax crayon to take rubbings of unusual textures
and patterns.

When you go out, take a sketchbook with you and make
small drawings of any interesting things you see.

At home you could turn some of
your ideas into paintings and
mount an exhibition.

Index

Broadbent, Tyrrel 35
Bruegel, Pieter (The Elder) 31

Canaletto 30
Caravaggio 15
Cassatt, Mary 21
cave painting 38
Chagall, Marc 8

Degas, Edgar 8

Egyptian paintings 14
Eisen, Keisai 23
Ernst, Max 26
Escher, Maurits 37
Eyck, Jan van 22

Ghirlandaio, Domenico 9
Gogh, Vincent van 24

Hobbema, Meindert 30
Hogarth, William 11

Indian painting 36

Japanese paintings 23
"Johannes" 32

Lawrence, Thomas 9
Leonardo da Vinci 8

Marc, Franz 20
Martineau, Robert 9
Michelangelo 39
Minoan painting 38
Morisot, Berthe 24

Picabia, Francis 34
Picasso, Pablo 15, 17

Pollock, Jackson 26

Raphael 29
Rembrandt van Rijn 12
Renoir, Auguste 24
Rubens, Peter Paul 40–1

Seurat, Georges 19
Steen, Jan 10

Tintoretto, Jacopo 29
Turner, Joseph (J.M.W.) 28

Velazquez, Diego 16
Vermeer, Jan 22, 23

wall paintings 38
Watteau, Antoine 32, 33
Whistler, James 21

Acknowledgments

The publishers would like to thank the following for kindly supplying photographs for this book:

Cover: Visual Arts Library, National Gallery of Art, Washington – Harris Whittemore Collection.
Page 8 Giraudon left, Visual Arts Library right, Cliché Musées Nationaux, Paris bottom left; 9 Tate Gallery, London top, Ashmolean Museum, Oxford/Visual Arts Library bottom left, Lambton Castle, Durham/Bridgeman Art Library bottom right; 10 Rijksmuseum, Amsterdam; 11 National Gallery, London; 12 Rijksmuseum, Amsterdam; 14 both pictures Michael Holford; 15 Tate Gallery, London (private collection) top, Fotomas Index/National Gallery, London bottom; 16 Madrid Prado/SCALA; 17 Museo Picasso de Barcelona; 19 Chicago Institute of Art, USA/Bridgeman Art Library; 20 Galerie Otto Stangl, Briennerstrasse/Städtische Galerie im Lenbachhaus, München; 21 *The White Girl (Symphony in White No 1)* – James McNeill Whistler, National Gallery of Art, Washington – Harris Whittemore Collection top; *The Boating Party*, Mary Cassatt, National Gallery of Art, Washington – Chester Dale Collection; 22 National Gallery, London top, Kunsthistorisches Museum, Vienna bottom; 23 both pictures Christie's, London; 24 Giraudon top, Christie's, London/ Bridgeman Art Library bottom right, S Kramarsky Trust Fund, New York bottom left; 26 Visual Arts Library; 28 Tate Gallery, London; 29 Louvre, Paris/Scala top, National Gallery, London bottom; 30 National Gallery, London top, Fotomas Index/National Gallery, London bottom; 31 Kunsthistorisches Museum, Vienna; 32 Bodleian Library, Oxford (Ms Bodley 264, fol 218R); 33 Reproduced by permission of the Trustees, The Wallace Collection, London; 34 Visual Arts Library; 35 Tyrrel Broadbent; 36 Michael Holford; 37 Ballantine Books Inc; 38 Michael Holford top, SCALA middle, Marion & Tony Morrison bottom; 39 SCALA; 41 National Gallery, London/ Visual Arts Library.

Special thanks to Alex and Catherine Rice for their pictures on pages 8, 11 and 18.
Picture Research: Sarah Donald